The Licensing Guru

The Licensing Guru

Simple Principles for Understanding
Microsoft Licensing

By J. H. Lara

2010 edition

"To Yolanda for her immense patience ...

And to the special people who encourage me to write this."

Preface

Microsoft has developed a complex way to distribute the rights of use of its software. Microsoft licensing is, for many IT and procurement professionals, a critical, dispassionate, ugly, and frustrating subject to deal with. In many meetings, I have heard constantly the following expressions in reference to this subject: black art, a nightmare, clear as mud, Greek to me. Overall, Microsoft licensing programs have earned a bad reputation within the IT world, increasing the criticism toward Microsoft as a well-oiled money machine that also leverages the complexity of the licensing offerings to gain at the expense of misinformed clients. IT and procurement professionals are not licensing professionals or lawyers, and they don't have the time or resources to keep track of licensing changes.

Microsoft licensing, thus, becomes a real problem—one you cannot escape because you use the products heavily or because it is the standard in your industry. You need to be informed either because you actually like the software or because, suddenly, Microsoft can call you to verify that you are compliant with your software installations.

If you are in the situation of dealing with Microsoft licensing, the first thing I need to tell you is:

Draw a line in the sand. Don't look at the past; concentrate on the present and prepare for the future.

Because I happen to be one of the very few people in this world who actually loves to know and talk about Microsoft licensing, people have renamed me the Licensing Guru, a title not completely earned in my opinion, but one that gives a sense of what I try to accomplish: to shed light on the darkness of Microsoft licensing, and to provide valuable advice and help to take this subject off of your black list. The notes you will read in the following pages correspond to the first semester of 2010. Microsoft licensing changes often, and I will try to update this book to reflect changes in the future.

Henceforth, I will try to explain a few ideas and concepts that will help you to start dealing with the situation and help you learn what you should basically know to confront the problem. Hopefully, you will be able to achieve the most cost-effective (cheapest) way to acquire your software, use the latest technology at all times, adapt deployments to your schedule, forecast accurately, and ensure compliance—in other words, hopefully you will achieve the desired and well-deserved licensing karma.

Sincerely,
The Licensing Guru

Contents

PART I

The Foundation

What Is out There: Types of Licenses

I think it's best to start by identifying the different types of licenses. I know it sounds very simple, but it's important to know the very basics, the foundation from which Microsoft builds the licensing programs. Be aware that this is "guru talk" here—it may not correspond to Microsoft-specific language.

There are two differentiators for licenses:

The commercial differentiation: the way Microsoft differentiates how you buy your licenses.

The technical differentiation: the way Microsoft allows you to use the software.

In the commercial differentiation, we find, essentially, the following:

> ➢ Full Product Package (Retail) licenses: this entails going to your favorite electronics store and buying a box that says "Office," for example. This contains a media CD/DVD for installation and a product key for that particular media. If you are In a license agreement, even a very small one with at least five desktops or users, stop buying this way right now! There are other ways for you. Nevertheless, if you are a commercial user (for example buying for personal use), this is the only way. Students also enjoy a discounted retail line of products.

> ➢ OEM (Original Equipment Manufacturer) license: as you know, in Microsoft's perfect world, there are no computers in the world manufactured without an operating system (such as Windows), and most of them contain a Windows license. Well, the reality is, if you want to buy a PC, most probably it will come with one of those. The one operating system that does not exist in the Microsoft world is Linux, so be aware that

Linux is a taboo word that opens the gates of the hell of compliance issues.

➢ Volume Licensing: these are software licenses acquired through licensing programs or agreements, including subscription licenses, hosted solutions, or other forms of licensing programs.

In the technical differentiation, we find the following:

➢ Operating System (OS): an example of this is Windows for the desktop or the server. This is the base on which all applications must be installed. Therefore, when an application is installed on an OS other than Windows, you must be careful that the gates of compliance hell do not open before you. Microsoft does not recognize many people who choose not to "be a PC," so they only offer a few applications that do not need a Windows OS (e.g., Office for Mac).

➢ Desktop Applications: This is for the software that sets on the desktop OS and is used for your financing, internet navigation, calendar tracking, and other purposes. One of the most important ones is Office, especially for licensing purposes in different agreement programs.

➢ Server Applications: This is for applications for your e-mail, filing, communications, or any other purpose that sits on top of an OS. As an example, the most popular ones are Microsoft Exchange Server and Microsoft SharePoint Server.

➢ CALs (Client Access Licenses): These are my favorites because these are subject to tremendous debate. CALs do not correspond to any tangible software application, they simply entail the right of the interaction between a desktop application and the server application. It does not really exist—in some cases, you just need to activate them; in some others you don't. Many people get confused about the actual need to have them. If you use any sort of server application, you *must* have them (with very few exceptions). These are my favorites because you cannot feel them, see them, or understand the need to pay not only for the server application but for the right to use it. Nevertheless, there they are, incomprehensibly attached to your licensing structure and becoming, perhaps, the most crucial part of your investments in software.

- o Exceptions: few products can be licensed either per processor (allowing unlimited access to the applications they offer) or per server. SQL can be licensed per processor, so you can avoid the cost of the CALs if you have many to acquire. Also, for internet-related sites, because it's impossible to know how many people can access the portal, Microsoft offers "External Connector," "web," and "Internet" licenses that will eliminate the need of CALs.

➤ Subscription Licenses: these licenses are essentially for rent. You don't own them, and you can use them only while your payment is valid. Microsoft has developed this licensing model for security software and also for other things like virtualization software on the desktop.

Also, you can find "cloud computing" licenses, the newest addition to the Microsoft licensing family. For example, License Productivity Online Suite (BPOSBusiness so it reads, Business Productivity Online Suite) with its Exchange, SharePoint, Office, System Center and other Hosted Services that gives you e-mail, document collaboration, Office applications, etc, through a web browser and is maintained by Microsoft and hosted on Microsoft's servers.

Google is a major enemy of Microsoft in terms of cloud computing. It is going to be interesting to see the development of Microsoft's offerings to compete against the free applications offered by Google.

Comment: most compliance issues occur when the wrong type of license is used. In many occasions, organizations do not realize they need to have a CAL that will allow them to be compliant on a server application's use. Also, a common mistake is to consider OEM licenses to be "volume licenses," and, consequently, you can make a mistake by reassigning the licenses when that is not part of the OEM rights.

If you are clear which type of licenses you need to use, then it is easier for you to decide which type of purchasing agreement or method you need with Microsoft.

Know Yourself: The Start

The very first thing to do in order to resolve your Microsoft licensing is to know yourself as a company in respect to your software use. Below are some questions that can help you to determine who you are:

What software do I critically use? It's very important to know if you use Windows, Office, Windows Server CAL, Exchange, and any other license that can determine which program or agreement you should aim for.

How often do I buy new editions? This question is critical to determine whether you should engage your licensing in the maintenance program (software assurance) or not. Also, it's important to verify whether you are losing productivity because of incompatibilities or lack of support for old technologies.

Do I want to be using the latest technology as often as possible? This question can also identify your cycle of refreshment of licenses. Do you care to be one edition behind or three editions behind? Lately, Microsoft seems to release a new edition every 24 to 30 months.

Am I planning to adopt new technologies? Which ones? If you are changing the tools you use, you need to consider how your environment is going to change and how your licenses will be affected. Many people forget to include the licensing repercussions in their projects and suddenly realize that the cost of the licensing is higher than the project implementation itself. Even the implementation of non-Microsoft products can affect the Microsoft Licensing. Thus, it's important to understand (in terms of other software manufacturers) the implications with respect to Microsoft licenses.

How much can I afford? This is a key question, especially in tumultuous economic times. Do you need to maintain cash flow? There are many ways to pay for licenses, and there are ways to fix costs over a term.

Do I have enough Knowledge? Most probably, if you need help it can be provided from two sources: Microsoft (directly) or a Microsoft partner. If you ask me—as a guru—it's better to rely on a partner who knows where to ask questions and how to approach Microsoft, one who has easy access to a licensing expert or an established relationship with Microsoft sales teams. Read the *Walking Together* chapter to learn how to choose a partner.

Look at yourself in your "IT mirror" and understand that you can find a process and model to buy your licenses ... smile, there is light at the end of the tunnel.

Know Your Space: Understand Your Limitations.

Very well, you know yourself better. Now let us talk about the roads that are open before in terms of Microsoft offerings on volume licensing and we will leave behind full product (retail) because those options are simple and expensive.

Your space to play depends on the number of computers you have. The magic number is 200; (Microsoft establishes the minimum number of computers to access a volume license agreement in 250). However the cost of about 250 licenses on some agreements is lower than 200 licenses in others

There are two basic programs or agreements with Microsoft especially designed for small medium licensees: open license and open value.

Open License (or Open License) this is a two-year program; it's the essential entry of volume licensing acquisition. The minimum requirement is five licenses or one qualifier server license. Once you buy your order entry, you have an authorization number that will allow you to buy more software during the remaining term at the same price level. Thus, it offers lower costs than retail, allowing you to buy licenses with or without a maintenance program or software assurance (SA). At the end of the two years, if you have purchased any software assurance, you should renew it if you want to continue its benefits (see the software assurance chapter).

Pros: allows you to buy software assurance, the minimum requirements are low, and you can find hundreds of resellers that can compete for your license. It is ideal for really small licensees.

Cons: it's the shortest program in Microsoft volume licensing offerings. Consequently, software assurance only lasts for two years. It is the most expensive option compared to other volume licensing programs or agreements. If you use different resellers, you may end up with multiple open license authorization numbers to buy from, making it difficult to manage your assets.

Considerations: basically, if you are buying open license, you may still be paying too much, and this program does not offer a good strategic field to reduce the ownership costs of your software.

Open Value: the open value agreement is the first of the agreements that offers a three-year term. Licenses always include software assurance. Microsoft has also made available suites of products under this agreement that only benefited bigger customers before. You can either buy a perpetual right of the license, or you can subscribe to use it on an open value subscription agreement.

Company-wide: in this option, Microsoft offers a discount price when you standardize licenses on all your computers. It includes the platform option for desktop licenses that will ease management and offer a discount. You must purchase licenses for all qualified desktops.

Non-company-wide: offers flexibility on the quantities you want to license without the compromise of buying for all your desktops. The minimum requirement is five licenses or one per processor license.

Pros: software assurance lasts one year longer than open license. It has a very small order threshold to enter the agreement. It offers suites of products for CALs that are very attractive at their discount price. This agreement is ideal if you have fewer than 200 computers and you are projecting a major standardization of Microsoft products in your IT infrastructure. It also offers (through the software assurance benefits) the ability to spread the payment on annual transactions.

Cons: software assurance is a core component, so if you decide to buy a license under this agreement—even if it is a copy of MapPoint for your manager's girlfriend (if she is an employee)—you will have to include it. If you are close to two hundred computers, the price is not as attractive as other higher agreements.

Open Value Subscription: this is the same as open value; however, instead of buying perpetual licenses (you own the rights of use even if you stop paying for software assurance) you "rent" the use of the licenses. It is quite useful for operational versus capital costs. If you work in an industry in which employee fluctuation is high (or you change the total number of users by season) this option may help you to annually revise the number instead of locking down your quantities for three years. On this option, you will have to adopt the company wide option.

Select Agreement: as the open license agreement under a select agreement, you have the ability to choose purchasing licenses with or without software assurance. It lasts for three years. This agreement is maintained by a forecast of acquisitions—in other words, you have to buy during or at the beginning of the term of the agreement enough points. Microsoft has assigned a point value to each product; the select agreement is divided into three pools: servers, applications, and operating system. For the first level of pricing (level A), you need to achieve five hundred points per year (minimum) by buying licenses to continue having the ability to buy under the discounted price of the select agreement. If you fail to achieve the minimum annual points on your acquisitions in any of the pools, then the pool is terminated and you will not be able to acquire more licenses under that pool.

It has four price levels, depending on the points earned every three years:

A	1,500 points
B	12,000 points
C	30,000 points
D	75,000 points

If you accumulate points, you can move to a lower price level.

Pros: allows you to buy software assurance if you want to, including spread payment options (every twelve months). This agreement offers lower cost than open license (or open value if you compare the license with software assurance cost). It also offers easier management of licenses under a single agreement number. Select is a good option for decentralized purchasing. Affiliates can enroll and collaborate on the sum of points achieved.

Cons: it may be difficult to maintain the pool point requirements. Licenses with software assurance have a higher cost than the enterprise agreement.

A Large Account Reseller (LAR) is the only reseller able to deliver the agreement

IMPORTANT: This agreement's end of life is July 1, 2011, meaning that all select clients will have to renew under select plus after that date.

Select Plus: as the select agreement, it requires you to earn a minimum number of points per pool every year; however, the minimum requirement is to commit to an initial five hundred points (level A) acquisition. Then the pool will not be terminated if, in the subsequent year, there is no additional purchase—the pool will be on hold until another equivalent acquisition needs to be made. All software assurance will be in effect for thirty-six months from the moment you buy during the first three-year term. After that, you will renew in prorated bases so, at the end of your second agreement renewal cycle, all licenses have the same software assurance term. An LAR is the only reseller able to deliver the agreement.

Price level per point achievement per order entry:

A	500
B	4,000
C	10,000
D	25,000

If you accumulate points, you can move to a lower price level.

Pros: allows you to buy software assurance if you want to, including spread payment options (every twelve months). It has a lower cost than open license and it's easier to manage licenses under a single agreement number. Select is a good option for decentralized purchasing. Affiliates can enroll and collaborate on the sum of points achieved.

Cons: Every purchase of software assurance during the initial agreement term is for thirty-six months. The minimum purchase is based on points, making it a little costly to enroll unless you were already looking to buy quite a few software licenses on products for one of the pools.

Enterprise Agreement: the infamous enterprise agreement (EA) is the preferred method of licensing for Microsoft. It is a deal between you and Microsoft, and the LAR acts as advisor and licensing management support after the agreement has been signed. This agreement offers the lowest software assurance. It's a three-year term as well, and the minimum requirement is that you purchase one of three products for every computer you have or, at minimum, 250. At the beginning of this chapter, I mentioned that my magical number is 200 because an EA for 250 licenses may be less expensive than 180 or 200 licenses of open value, for example.

To have an EA, one of the following products, a combination of two of them, or all three must be licensed equal to your number of computers: Office, Windows OS and CALs (line of license application machines—such as cashier computers—or a hard drive with an embedded OS do not need to be counted for this requirement).

There are four price levels for qualifying computers:

A   250—2,399

B   2,400—5,999

C   6,000—14,999

D   15,000+

The agreement lasts for three years and can be renewed for a one- or three-year term thereafter. Software assurance is a core component of this agreement.

Price is fixed during the term.

You can license Office, Windows OS for the desktop, or CALs on their own, or you can license a combination of them.

If you license the three qualifying products, then you will receive an additional discount. They are considered EA full product platform. There are two suites of products that offer these full product platform desktop suites: Professional Deskop and Enterprise Desktop (Microsoft distinguishes between four, the before mentioned and also CAL suites: Core CAL and Enterprise. Microsoft can also add the Desktop Optimization Pack-MDOP-):

Professional desktop includes:

> ➢ Windows 7 Enterprise OS upgrade
> ➢ Office Professional Plus 2010
> ➢ Core CAL Suite

Enterprise desktop includes:

> ➢ Windows 7 Enterprise OS upgrade
> ➢ Office Professional Plus
> ➢ Office Enterprise 2010
> ➢ Core CAL Suite
> ➢ ECAL Suite

If you decide just to license CALs, you cannot license them individually; they must be licensed under CAL suites as the core CAL and the enterprise CAL*

Core CAL includes:

> ➢ Microsoft Windows Server CAL
> ➢ Microsoft Exchange Server CAL
> ➢ Microsoft Systems Management Server,
> ➢ Microsoft SharePoint Portal Server CAL

Enterprise CAL includes:

> ➢ Core CAL:
>   • Microsoft Windows Server CAL
>   • Microsoft Exchange Server CAL
>   • Microsoft Systems Management Server,
>   • Microsoft SharePoint Portal Server CAL
> ➢ Microsoft Exchange Server Enterprise CAL
> ➢ Microsoft Office SharePoint Server Enterprise CAL
> ➢ Microsoft Communications Server Standard CAL
> ➢ Microsoft Communications Server Enterprise CAL
> ➢ Microsoft Windows Rights Management Services CAL
> ➢ Microsoft Forefront Security Suite
> ➢ Microsoft Operations Manager Desktop Operations Management License (OML)

Also, on an EA, the only Office editions available are Office Pro Plus or higher, either by themselves or as part of the above mentioned desktop suites.

Once you have decided to license one, two, or three desktop licenses, then you can add any other product at any quantity you desire.

You can deploy products at any time during the term and report the increase of licenses used in an annual process called the "True Up."

There is a document called CPS (Customer Price Sheet) that is the critical document that will establish the licenses and costs for you during the term. It is revised and modified upon renewal. This document also establishes the cost of "True Up." It also contains "step up" fixed costs in case you desire a higher suite of products And, finally, it will include any exception or services Microsoft may offer to you. The negotiation of this CPS is the critical part, and the LAR should be helping you to understand the implications of the software licenses offered by Microsoft and how to maximize the investment. A deal may contain more than one CPS.

The lowest prices you find in the CPS are the ones that are negotiated as annual payments. This price is called "added at signing" for new licenses. "True Up" costs are considerably higher, so it is good to forecast your growth at the very beginning and, if you are confident, acquire the licenses on day one.

Enterprise Agreement Subscription: this is equal to the traditional enterprise agreement, but with the difference that, instead of being perpetual licenses (you own the rights of use even if you stop paying for software assurance), you "rent" the use of the licenses (you don't own the licenses when you stop paying the bill); if you desire, you can "buy" the licenses instead of renting them at a percentage cost when you decide. It is quite useful for operational versus capital costs. If you work in an industry in which employee fluctuation is high or you change the total number of users by season, this option may help you to annually revise the number—instead of locking down your quantities for three years.

Choosing the Path: The Key Question

So, after you know which space you can play, which agreement you can enroll under, you must ask yourself the crucial and difficult question, "Which path should I take?" As you can see, there are multiple paths—it's not a question of right or left. In fact, with Microsoft licensing, you can choose multiple paths simultaneously. You can even choose a path and have another as a backup.

How do you choose? Well, if you know yourself (as we have discussed before), then a critical question can be answered: how often you plan to upgrade editions of software. If you plan to skip one or two editions (and hopefully Microsoft will maintain a rate of a new edition every twenty-four to thirty months), this could mean that you upgrade licenses every four years. In this case, the investment in software assurance has to be considered because, in the long term, it will save you money.

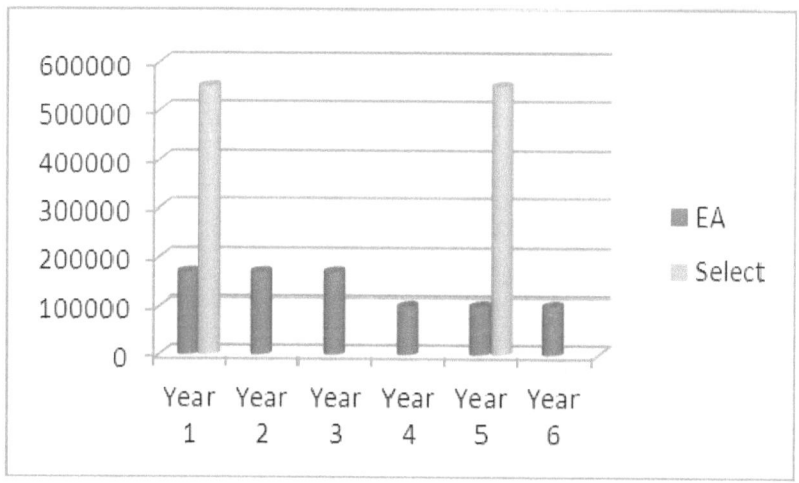

Now, if your upgrade of an edition for a license will take five years or beyond, then software assurance investment per costs alone is not going to work. The benefits may still be attractive; however, costs will not be lower. So a non–software assurance scenario could be more suitable for you.

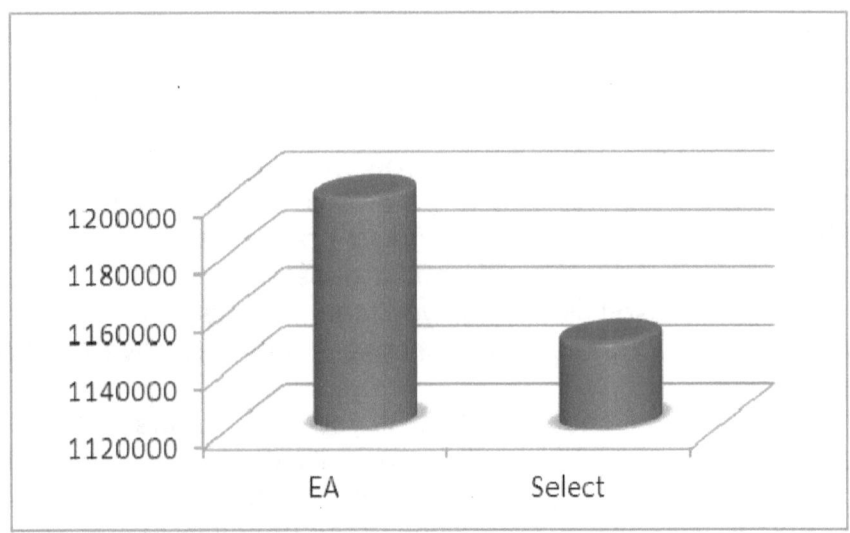

As mentioned before, you can take different paths. So, for different licenses, you can choose one path with software assurance and another without. Let me give you an example:

Company A, with three hundred desktops, wants to be able to have support and be current on the latest or almost the latest technology (skipping one edition) with the server products and CALs. It's going to acquire upgrade licenses for the Windows OEM. They currently run Windows XP and want to use Windows 7. The company does not anticipate upgrading Windows for five to seven years.

After looking at cost options for select and enterprise agreement, company A decides to go with an EA for core CAL suite and other server licenses; it determines that a select agreement just for Windows upgrade licenses without software assurance will match their Windows upgrade plans. The company understands that they will not qualify on the second year for the OS pool on select, but they are OK with that fact because, in the first year, they will be able to buy the licenses at the select discounted price. If the Windows acquisition has enough points, they will complete the transaction under select plus to avoid pool cancellation.

Because you know yourself, you know that some of the software assurance benefits could be of interest. Let us imagine that, for your organization, it's critical to maintain cash flow, and you want to make sure you use the spread payment option of software assurance. You may desire to change your upgrade cycle of licenses to make it worth the investment on software assurance and make sure that you can pay (annually) a lower amount than you paid upfront.

You may believe that an Office upgrade is necessary, but you are concerned that the transition for the new users from a very old Office edition to the latest and fanciest one will be difficult. Then you want to use the software assurance benefit, home use program, so people will have the software for their personal use and they will also get online training from the E-learning benefit included in Software Assurance.

If you require decentralized purchasing and you have around two hundred computers, it may be wise to choose the select/select plus agreement because it's more flexible on affiliates and quantities, and you will probably meet the point requirements. Otherwise, open license is your solution.

If you require standardization of all your users or desktops at once, then contemplate the possibility of reduced costs of licenses under open value or enterprise agreements.

Here are some key points to help you decide which agreement you need:

If you have less than 200 or 250 computers you can choose open license or open value.

If you have more than 200 or 250 computers, you can evaluate enterprise agreement or select/select plus options.

For educational institutions: If you require standardization and the ability to upgrade without additional costs, campus or school agreement is your solution. Otherwise, select or open license is a good option.

In the cloud computing—Software as a Service (SaaS)

Get ready for commercial war. With netbooks and other devices out there, Microsoft competes heavily with other providers of software that are allocating the applications "in the cloud" accessed by subscription licenses. The offer of applications accessed online will be greater in the near future.

In the Microsoft perspective, if you own the applications already and have CALs to use them as well, then they acknowledge the investment and the subscription rates are reduced (if you own software assurance).

As of today, the Microsoft offerings are part of the licensing called Business Productivity Online Suite. It is increasing its offerings, and it can be a very interesting way to license your software needs. I believe we will be licensed this way in the future.

Software Assurance

The software assurance (SA) benefits are the "maintenance" program of Microsoft and offer one very important benefit: the right to upgrade your software at no additional cost. These rights are also known as new version rights. The amount of SA benefits received with your purchase depends on the products and the quantities. The more you buy, the more benefits you get; consequently, agreements like EA offer more benefits than some purchases under select or open value.

The software assurance benefits (in "guru-talking" form) are:

> New version rights: the ability to upgrade (always) to the latest edition of the software.
> Spread payment: the ability to split the cost of the agreement over the term of the license and SA into annual payments (or prorated payments every six months for additional purchases of education agreements).
> 24x7 support: the ability to report incidents to Microsoft and utilize their support resources; normally 24-hour response in the form of an answer, not onsite support.
> Home use program: this allows your employees to run a product at home for any purpose. The software is compliant only while the employee is part of your organization. Normally, this benefit is for the Office suite.
> Cold Backup: a great option for disaster recovery; it allows licenses with SA to be deployed in the inactive servers on a separate cluster with no obligation to buy more licenses for that same server license.
> Employee Purchase:. this benefit allows your employees to buy software from Microsoft at a supposed discount price. The product offerings also include entertainment. This is about to disappear.
> Source Code: it provides you with Windows source code for your development projects.
> Hotfix Support: it saves you money if you have support contracted from Microsoft and also provides certain products with hotfixes.

➢ MDOP (Microsoft Desktop Optimization Pack): this is considered a benefit, though it is a subscription to be paid as well. If you have SA, you can add this subscription, which contains management tools and, probably its most important feature, application virtualization.

➢ Multi-language pack: this allows you to deploy your office license in various languages.

➢ Packaged services: this benefit is a very important one, often overlooked by 'Microsoft's clients. Basically, these are dollars that Microsoft gives you to do assessments—Exchange, desktop deployment, or 'SharePoint, for example. One day of services is approximately equal to one thousand dollars, and decreases in value the more you use do a specific assessment. To use this benefit, you need to contact a large account reseller (LAR) or qualified partner that has the services you require—good luck, most LARs are purely transactional, and if they don't talk to you about these services when you sign the agreement, it's because they cannot redeem this money for you.

➢ Step up: some products have a special rate to change your edition to a higher one, this benefit allows you to make an acquisition at a lower cost than if you were to buy a full upgrade.

➢ TechNet: this is access to technical information to help you resolve problems or learn about the technologies, including trial downloads.

➢ Windows fundamentals for legacy PCs: basically, this is Windows XP SP2 that will help you to have an OS on very old computers.

➢ Windows 7 enterprise: if you buy Windows OS for the desktop with SA, then you can deploy the enterprise edition instead of the standard edition.

It is crucial to understand whether SA is of value to you or not.

If it's not, your options are OEM, retail, open license, select and select plus.

If it is, your options are OEM+SA (within ninety days of hardware acquisition), open value, select or select plus, and enterprise agreement.

Evidently, Microsoft wants you to buy software assurance so you will face the following reality regarding the licensing options:

> ➢ All the product suites: core CAL, enterprise CAL, professional desktop or enterprise desktop contain software assurance as a core component.
> ➢ Some additional products like MDOP are only available or highly discounted with software assurance.

Because you will confront this reality, it's very important to know from your reseller the benefits for the software options you are contemplating. The resellers can calculate the benefits you will get for the operation.

Real Life: Negotiating Your Agreement.

So far we have discussed the "letter of the law" regarding types of licenses and program agreements. However, real life can be somewhat different. And this is because Microsoft divides its company into regions, and these regions may allow exceptions depending on their own market needs or other circumstances. Some products contain different features in different parts of the globe. And this is a good thing; it shows us that Microsoft can be quite flexible.

First of all, do not expect to negotiate unless you are a valuable catch. If you are going to acquire open license, for example, no one will consider special terms and conditions for you; you must be eligible for higher agreements.

If you are a good catch (meaning that you qualify for select or EA), then you can talk to your Microsoft representative in your region and the LAR and discuss how to make things work to get the software you need at reasonable, lower cost and adjust terms to your company's standards

EA is the agreement that offers the most flexibility. As it is a deal between you and Microsoft directly, there is no reseller marking up the cost for a profit margin. This means that Microsoft can establish price discounts or levels without having to respond to another party. It also means that there is no LAR who can modify costs (beware of LARs who say they can get you an EA at a better price than another, it is a lie).

EA (and sometimes select) terms and conditions can be modified through amendments.

What follows are some examples of things I have witnessed in the licensing world that you may want to consider when negotiating your agreement. Remember that the flexibility that Microsoft exhibits with the following points depends on the size of your organization and the potential deal.

> *Existing Software:* you may have already purchased software in another agreement. Microsoft is able to transfer the license to your new agreement if you own

SA on the licenses. If you don't own SA, the first response to a transfer from your agreement request will be *no*; however, you may receive an option to retroactively buy SA for the existing licenses to add them into your new agreement.

➢ *Components of the desktop on EA:* remember that you can either license the pro desktop or enterprise desktop suites on your EA, or you can choose only components. Some LARs forget to tell you that you are only required to buy Office, CALs, or Windows (or a combination of them equal to your number of computers). It is not an obligation to buy all three of them. At the same time, sometimes the LAR will omit to explain to you the discount prices if you license the full platform.

➢ *Close to level breakpoint:* you may be very close to a price level breakpoint. Microsoft may amend your agreement so you can take advantage of the better price level.

➢ *Upfront payment on EA:* if you prefer to pay upfront for the three years of the term, Microsoft may amend your agreement to be able to do so.

➢ *Agreement umbrella:* if you are an affiliate or belong to a bigger firm that has an existing agreement, you can request that Microsoft creates an agreement for you that reflects that relationship—i.e., you would enjoy the same price level and would not be subject to the same minimum requirements (like select or select plus pool points requirement).

➢ *Microsoft engagement on projects:* you can test the waters on the level of commitment Microsoft can dedicate to your projects. You can receive either resources or even funds for specific technology transitions from competitors or the deployment of new technologies that can serve Microsoft as a case study.

➤ *Assessments:* out of the SA benefits you may receive assessments to help your IT infrastructure be more dynamic.

➤ *Affiliate considerations:* you can allow affiliates to enroll; however, your definition of affiliate may be different than what Microsoft states in the agreement documentation. Microsoft may amend the agreement to allow your affiliates to enroll under your umbrella and enjoy your price, terms, and conditions.

➤ *Term period:* In rare cases (though it is possible), Microsoft may allow you to have a different term for the expiration of your agreement.

➤ *Re-write your EA:* you may be confronting a huge True Up due to a merge or acquisition, and Microsoft may allow you to sign a new EA that will give you the advantage of committing to annual payments instead of upfront True Up payments for the additional licenses and obtain the discount price of the licenses "added at signing." This could help you as well to add an existing agreement to yours.

➤ *Desktop exceptions:* if some of your desktops don't use certain components of the suites you are interested in or you require different editions, Microsoft may allow you to have some of the desktop count that qualifies for Enterprise agreement exempt to be licensed for all the components of the suite, especially if some line of licensed desktops need certain products of the suites.

➤ *Minimum point qualification:* Microsoft could approve an amendment to allow you to achieve the minimum point required for select plus within the first twelve months.

There may be other exemptions and interesting cases, I will try to update this content with relevant information in future editions.

Comment: Ask, ask, and ask. Asking is very important. Either you or your reliable partner reseller should ask and talk to Microsoft to know how flexible they can be with your conditions. Of course, the more you demand, the more you should expect

Microsoft to ask you to get more technology suites. Also, talk to your peers: if they have obtained certain benefits in your area then, most probably, those same benefits can be extended to you.

Beware of country of use of your licenses. Normally, where your organization's headquarter is located is where your agreement is signed. You may determine to sign an agreement in a different location due to a price difference; however, you may lose all negotiating advantages or support from Microsoft and a reliable LAR. There is real value in the services offered in a good partnership.

Walking Together: The Search for the Right Partner.

If you want an EA or select, the actors in the negotiation are the 'Microsoft' representative, the LAR, and you, of course. If you want to have in place other agreements, you can also select a value added reseller (VAR).

It seems strange that when there is a deal between you and Microsoft an LAR is involved. The LAR is a Microsoft partner who processes the paperwork and transaction. The role of the LAR should be to guide you to understand all the licensing implications of your software and projects, give you tips on how to talk the Microsoft language, propose solutions before Microsoft starts negotiating, and manage the agreement after it is signed, helping you to maximize the investment and guide you on the services you may need.

The LAR is responsible (as far as Microsoft is concerned) to ensure that you're aware of all the reasons to renew your investment, to make you happy with the EA, to help you comprehend the implications of your projects on licensing, and to offer you advice on how to avoid incompliance situations.

On the EA, you don't pay the LAR—Microsoft provides the fee as a broker service. Part of the fees given to the LAR could cover the LAR's cost to help you with software asset management, for example. You should always ask your LAR what value he or she is going to bring to the table.

Any dummy can process an order, but to support you with services or offer you additional support for your IT infrastructure (either providing assessments of projects or reliable information sources) should be a key value of the LAR professionals. The LAR should have the responsibility to advise you throughout your licensing investment process. The LAR should also help you understand your environment.

Comments: Good luck finding an LAR who can do everything I've mentioned in your region. I encourage you to contact "the guru" for guidance.

Microsoft understands that the LAR community needs to do something more than just process orders. Historically, LARs have offered very little value to clients. Lately, though, the strategies and market approach are changing and LARs are adapting.

PART II

The Architecture

Putting the Puzzle Together: Licensing Scenarios

If you have this book in your hands, it is because you have scratched your head trying to understand how licensing works. You may already be familiar with purchasing options; you may even have an agreement in place with Microsoft already. Now the problem is figuring out how licensing works so you don't receive just poor advice that can put you on the road to incompliance or cause you to buy more than what you need.

In this chapter, I want to review some examples of common licensing scenarios. The scenarios are based on common questions one might face when trying to help organizations with their projects. There may be different ways to license the software, but there are fixed rules on how to build the licensing architecture correctly. There are use rights that also affect the way you choose a license and, of course, there are different types of licenses for a single product.

There is a common premise: every device needs to run a Microsoft operating system (OS). Based on this premise, we will build all the following licensing scenarios.

OEM

The OEM licenses cannot be transferred from one computer to another; they "die with the hardware." It is also important to mention that in Microsoft's perfect world, there is no computer that leaves the factory without an OS. This means that if you purchase a "white box" computer (without an OS or with Linux), you cannot buy an OEM license or buy an upgrade license on any volume licensing program—just retail. It is mandatory to have a qualifying OS according to Microsoft.

I have seen many companies that consider OEM licenses to be assets they can allocate to a different computer once the original one dies. This is a common mistake for Office OEM licenses. OEM cannot be reassigned to a different computer.

There is a way to get around this problem. If you just purchase the hardware with the OEM license, you can add SA to the OEM license within ninety days. The SA can be reassigned, and this allows you to get free new editions for the OEM license. This may be a good strategy when refreshing your hardware. The SA can be acquired under any volume licensing program agreement you desire that fulfills the minimum qualifications for that agreement.

Adding SA to the OEM licenses can also be useful if you are looking to add licenses that are exclusively offered (or highly discounted) if you have SA, such as MDOP.

Obviously, if OEM must come with your computer, the Windows license you buy under volume licensing is not a full license but, rather, an upgrade. This is important to note because, if you are offered to buy Windows under volume licensing, you probably will feel like you are paying twice for it (this is a feeling I can sympathize with), but technically you are not—you are upgrading your license to have rights of reassignment, more flexible imaging rights (depending on the edition), use of a single key, and a better ability to do virtual instances and/or use SA benefits.

File Servers

Let us start with the basic function of servers: filling.

Licenses needed:

Windows Server

Windows OS for the user computer

Windows Server CAL

The licensing architecture is as follows:

E-mail

For the use of exchange servers and other server applications, the basic architecture of a Windows server OS must already exist.

Licenses needed:

Windows Server

Windows OS for the user computer

Windows Server CAL

Exchange Server license (Enterprise or Standard)

Exchange Server CAL (Standard)

The Licensing architecture is as follows:

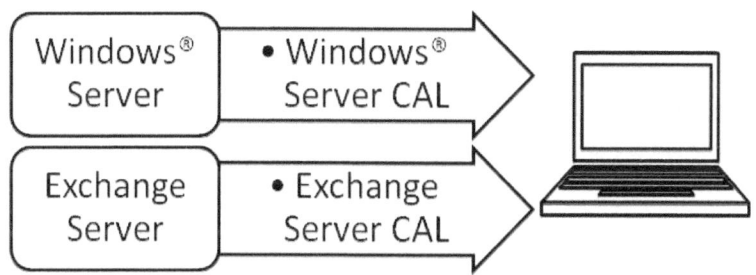

If you choose the use of an exchange enterprise server to extend the limitations of e-mail capabilities, you will only need an exchange standard CAL unless you use the features of unified communications.

CALs are like love (here I'm speaking as the guru). CALs are intangible and abstract, once you use their licensing power you cannot operate without them.

As mentioned in chapter 1, CALs are required for the use of server applications. Combinations of CALs are required to make sure you are compliant in the access of products that build a single technology.

To use the Outlook web access feature (the ability to look at your Outlook from the exchange server on a web browser), you are only required to have the Exchange CAL.

Server Virtualization

It is important to understand the correct way to license the server OS in the virtualization environment.

Windows Server Standard offers one install per server.

Windows Server Enterprise offers one install per server and four virtual instances of the OS.

Windows Server Datacenter is licensed per processor (CPU socket), offering unlimited virtual instances of the OS.

A virtual server is considered to be another individual server and, consequently, additional licenses are required for server applications running on them unless the server license is used in a disaster recovery scenario and the second install of the server is in inactive mode.

Regardless of the manufacturer's technology you use to virtualize your systems, the same Microsoft rules apply.

Examples of the licensing architecture:

Server virtualization

With Windows Server Enterprise

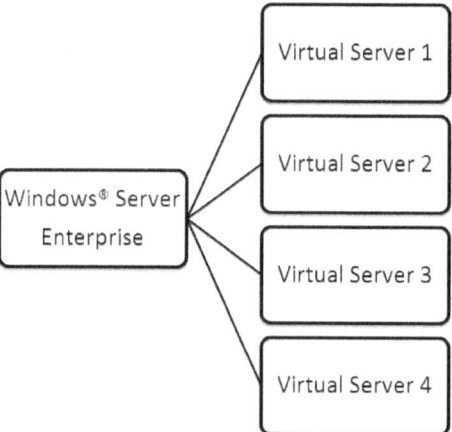

With Windows Server Data Center

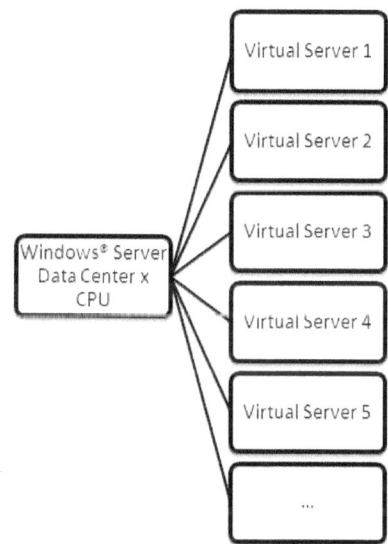

Desktop Virtualization

It is more and more common to find organizations looking to use the virtualization power on the desktop, either using multiple instances of the OS on the same computer (e.g., shift work computers) or streaming the OS from the server to any device (e.g., hospital terminals where doctors and nurses can access their running OS and applications in any patient's room).

You could be looking to virtualize the applications so you can run two editions at the same time or for failover precaution. There are many reasons you might choose virtualization and engage with other non-Microsoft virtual engines. Again, regardless of the manufacturer you use to virtualize your systems, the same Microsoft rules apply.

Let us review how it is licensed.

If you are looking to virtualize your desktops OS on the same hardware, please be aware that Windows 7 Enterprise edition (only available with software assurance) will allow you to create up to four virtual instances.

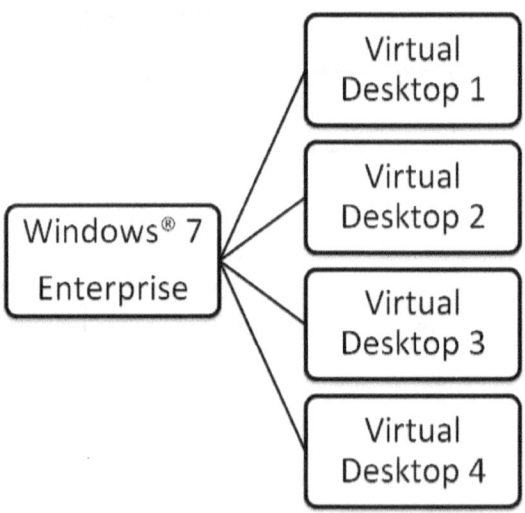

You may be looking to stream the OS image from the server. In this case, you will need the following licenses:

Windows Server

Windows 7 OS with SA for computer

Windows Server CAL

Remote Desktop Services CAL (the new name for the Terminal Server CAL)

Remote Desktop Services CALs or Terminal Server CALs help you to remotely access the content of your servers and the content of your desktop because of their virtual desktop infrastructure feature.

As of July 2010 you are not required to buy a subscription for OS virtualization, only MDOP if you require application virtualization.

Do not mistake thinking this is a substitute for CALs needed to run the applications; you will still need to have all necessary support CALs or application licenses.

It Is Important to notice that if your Remote Desktop Services CALs are licensed with Software Assurance you will also own the feature for application Virtualization App-V that will allow you to stream the virtual instance of the additional applications you want to run (e.g., Excel).

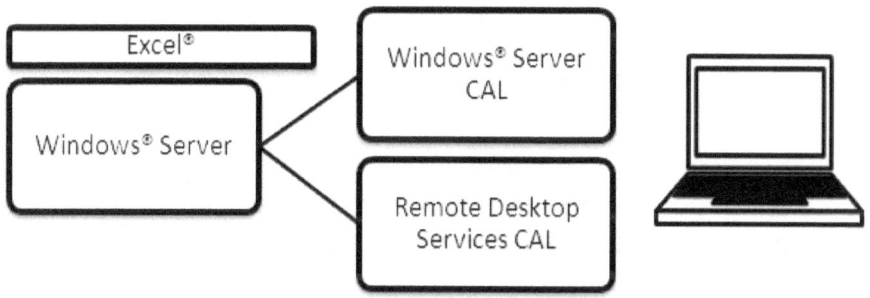

Application Virtualization on the desktop.

To do application virtualization on the desktop you need to license your OS to be able to do the virtualization with an additional subscription license called MDOP (Microsoft Desktop Optimization Pack). MDOP contains many features—the most significant for many people is the application virtualization App-V that came from the SoftGrid acquisition that Microsoft made. So, if you subscribed to SoftGrid, your new license edition is MDOP. Interestingly, you will have to consider having the OS with software assurance to acquire MDOP. So, even if you have an OEM license, most probably you will need to buy a volume license for the OS or add SA to a new purchased computer with OEM within ninety days.

The Licensing Architecture is as follows:

Windows OS for the user computer

MDOP subscription per computer

Application(s) license(s) (in this example, Excel 2003, Excel 2007)

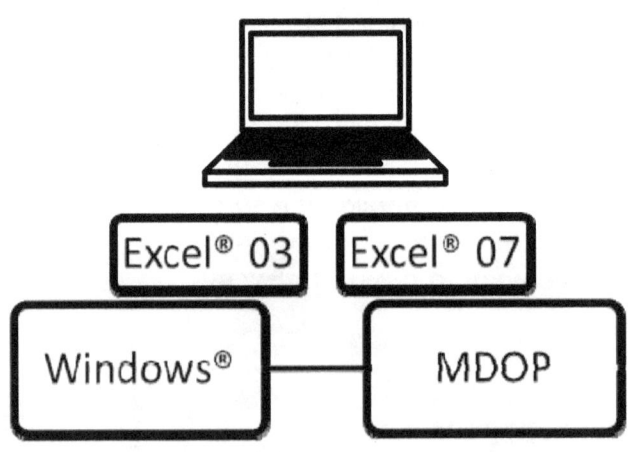

The use of downgrade rights will prevent you from purchasing additional licenses for the same application; just make sure you are able to downgrade to the edition you desire with the right media.

Document Management and Databases (SharePoint and SQL)

Many organizations need document management and intranet portals for collaboration. SharePoint has different editions according to the features you want to use; nevertheless, the architecture is the same.

SQL can be the database application you use to support your documents and files content and search.

The licensing architecture is as follows:

Windows Server

Windows OS for the user computer

Windows Server CAL

SharePoint Server (Enterprise or Standard)

SharePoint Server CAL (Enterprise or Standard)

If you build a SharePoint Database you can license SQL with it, it can be licensed per server with CALs for all users accessing it, or it can be licensed per processor giving you the flexibility to have unlimited users accessing the database—this is especially useful if the processor cost is lower than buying SQL CALs for all your users.

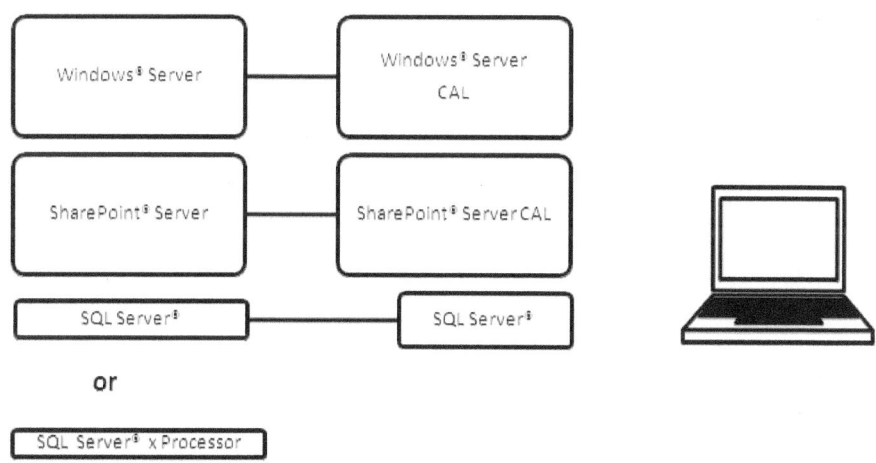

You may, however, want to create a portal for clients or partners of your License that will gain access through the "cloud." If that is the case, then you should license it in a different way:

Windows Server

External Connector

SharePoint External Connector

And if you use SQL Server for SharePoint database interaction, then you will need the SQL Server per processor license. Obviously, you will need the application licenses that will interact with SharePoint.

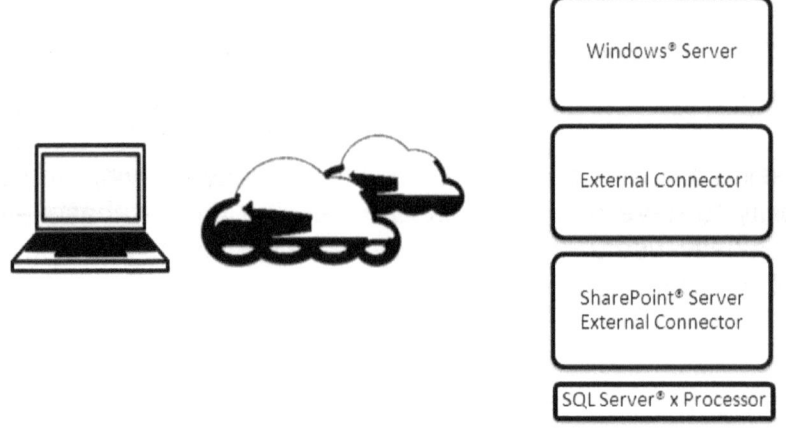

Unified Communications

To run unified communications that include e-mail, instant messaging with presence, voice mail, and phone capabilities, you will need an Exchange Server Enterprise License that will set upon the Windows Server Standard, Enterprise, or Data Center license and an Office Communicator Server Enterprise and Standard License with a Communicator License (part of Office Pro Plus).

Consequently, you will need the following:

CALs:

> Windows Server CAL
> Exchange Server Enterprise CAL (in the top of the Exchange Server Standard CAL)
> Office Communicator Server Standard CAL
> Office Communicator Server Enterprise CAL
> Voice CAL (as of May 2010, Microsoft has announced that this CAL will be a new, separate component) if voice capabilities are required

Applications:

> Windows Server
> Exchange Enterprise Server
> Exchange Standard Server
> Office Communicator Server Enterprise
> Office Communicator Server Standard
> Office Professional Plus (for communicator license)

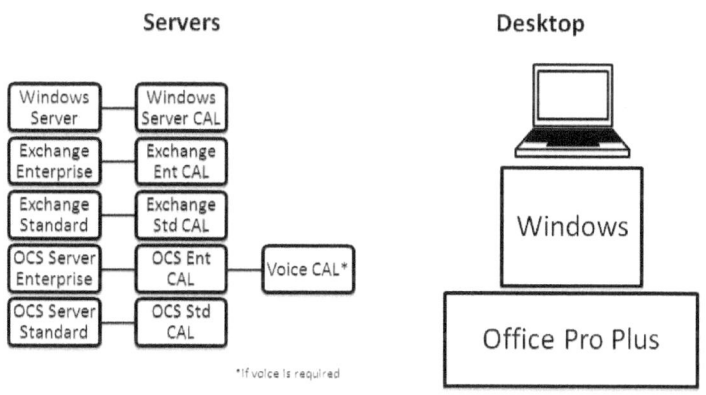

Let us imagine that you want to extend the unified messaging capabilities to external resources to your network. You will need public instant messaging licenses for those users.

If you are interested only in presence and instant messaging (but not in voice or full interaction with Exchange), then you will need the following:

- ➢ Windows Server
- ➢ Exchange Server Standard
- ➢ Office Communicator Server Standard
- ➢ Office Professional Plus (for Communicator license)

Unified communications have definitely increased in use, and they are already implemented in many organizations. If you already own a phone system or unified communications system, I encourage you to contact a certified service company to explain to you how to use the technologies available and how your licenses can be combined with your current communications structure.

Final Remarks

Clear as mud? You may have to revisit these pages again and again, but hopefully you have clarified enough basic points to achieve your perfect licensing architecture. Maybe you will feel less confused looking at the Microsoft online resources. I encourage you to download the freely available product use right document and have a licensing specialist explain the details if necessary.

The path to compliance redemption or an adequate "licensing lifestyle" is like everything in life: full of variables. Make sure you engage the right partner to help you understand licensing, because no one can be isolated—we are social beings, and we need each other when we confront the unknown.

Microsoft changes licensing constantly, and it is difficult to keep track of the changes as a normal IT professional whose main responsibility is to maintain, deploy, and develop. I encourage you to take a deep breath and go slowly as you explore licensing. Your timeline is the most important one. Achieving licensing karma is closer than you think.

There are multiple ways to be licensed; maybe a new cocktail of licensing options is adequate for you. Just make sure that there are no questions unanswered by Microsoft or its resellers.

I encourage you to "know yourself" and anticipate the licensing implications of your projects.

There is help out there in the form of qualified Microsoft employees and partners. It's always important to have a good software asset management tool to test your compliance from time to time. And remember that you can always fix things if you need to.

I appreciate you taking the time to read these words, and I hope that this book can be used as a reference for your licensing dealings.

Speaking as the guru, I hope that the complex will turn out to be simple and the simple will stay that way.

Sincerely,
The Licensing Guru

www.ingramcontent.com/pod-product-compliance
Lightning Source LLC
Chambersburg PA
CBHW021043180526
45163CB00005B/2265